torn pages repaired JP 9/1/15

DO YOU REALLY WANT TO VISIT MARS?

BY THOMAS K. ADAMSON

ILLUSTRATED BY DANIELE FABBRI

amicus
illustrated

Amicus Illustrated is published by Amicus
P.O. Box 1329, Mankato, MN 56002
www.amicuspublishing.us

Library of Congress Cataloging-in-Publication Data
Adamson, Thomas K., 1970–
Do you really want to visit Mars? / by Thomas K.
Adamson ; illustrated by Daniele Fabbri. — 1st ed.
    p. cm. — (Do you really want to visit—?)
Audience: K-3.
Summary: "A child astronaut takes an imaginary trip to
Mars, learns about the harsh conditions on the rocky
red planet, and decides that Earth is a good home after
all. Includes solar system diagram, Mars vs. Earth fact
chart, and glossary"—Provided by publisher.
 Includes bibliographical references.
 ISBN 978-1-60753-198-2 (library binding) —
ISBN 978-1-60753-403-7 (ebook)
1. Mars (Planet)—Juvenile literature. 2. Mars (Planet)—
Exploration—Juvenile literature. I. Fabbri, Daniele, 1978-
ill. II. Title. III. Series: Do you really want to visit—?
QB641.A328 2014
523.43—dc23   2012025972

Editor: Rebecca Glaser
Designer: The Design Lab

Printed in the United States of America at
Corporate Graphics in North Mankato, Minnesota.

Date 102113   PO 1181

9 8 7 6 5 4 3 2

Out of range again! If only you had a remote control car with the longest range ever—like a rover on Mars! It would be cool to go to Mars. But do you *really* want to go to there?

LUCKY

Mars is the fourth planet from the Sun.
It will take about 8 months to get there.
That's long enough to skip a grade!

When you land, you'll see why Mars is called the red planet. The ground is covered with rusty-orange dirt and rocks. Get your space suit and oxygen mask! Mars's thin air has little oxygen.

5

Walking around, you see a Mars rover heading over to a rusty rock. You can't change where it goes.

It's following directions sent from Earth. It scrapes the rock and scoops up dirt. The rover runs an experiment. It will send the data back to Earth.

You need something faster than a rover to get around the planet. Good thing you've got a hovercraft in your spaceship's loading bay. Now, off to explore!

A massive volcano looms in the distance. Olympus Mons is the largest volcano in the whole solar system. Its base is as big as Arizona. The volcano is so wide and tall you can't see the top from the ground.

10

Next, you fly to the biggest canyon in the solar system, Vallis Marineris. Several Grand Canyons could fit inside it. It's like a maze in here.

So far, Mars looks dry. But look at the poles. There's
ice here, but it's mostly carbon dioxide ice. Try digging.

Mars has water ice underground. But you can't just sweep away the dust and go skating. On the surface, the ice would disappear. Mars's thin atmosphere would cause the ice to evaporate, even at cold temperatures.

Uh-oh. There's a dust storm coming. This happens a lot on Mars. Sometimes a dust storm covers the whole planet. Better move out!

Let's get above this mess. You can visit one of Mars's two small, oddly shaped moons on your way out. They are probably asteroids that got close to Mars and are now orbiting it.

Phobos looks like a potato. It whips around Mars three times a day. And it's slowly falling toward the planet.

Don't worry. It won't happen for another 50 million years. Mars's other moon, Deimos, is farther away and even smaller.

But you're starting to miss Earth.
Mars is fine for a remote control rover...

. . . but it's too cold and dusty to visit for very long!

20

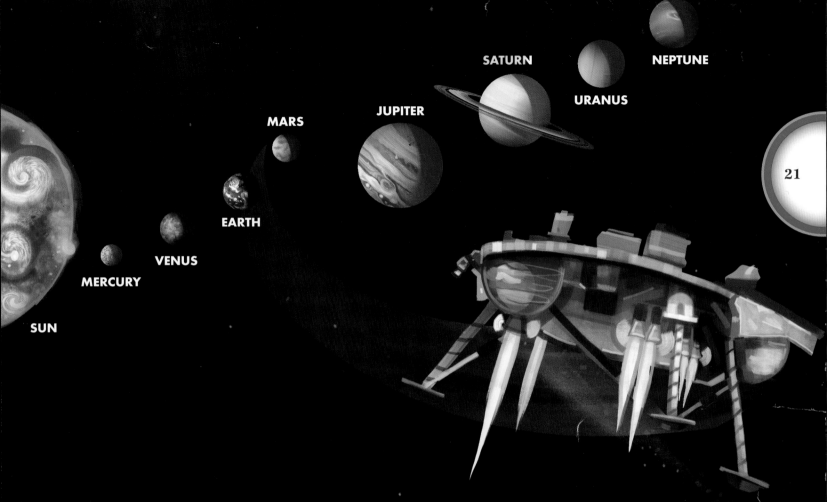

SUN
MERCURY
VENUS
EARTH
MARS
JUPITER
SATURN
URANUS
NEPTUNE

How Do We Know About Mars?

We can't actually go to Mars yet. But more spacecraft have explored Mars than any other planet. Two spacecraft are still in orbit around Mars, *Mars Odyssey* and *Mars Reconnaissance Orbiter*. Both crafts have mapped the surface and taken pictures. Robotic spacecraft have landed on Mars' surface. NASA landed *Curiosity*, a car-sized rover, on Mars in August 2012. It studied the soil and looked for signs of life on the planet.

Earth vs. Mars

	Earth	Mars
Position in solar system	Third from Sun	Fourth from Sun
Average distance from Sun	93 million miles (150 million km)	141.7 million miles (228 million km)
Year (time to orbit Sun)	365 days	687 days
Day (sunrise to sunrise)	24 hours	24 hours, 37 minutes
Diameter	7,926 miles (12, 756 km)	4,222 miles (6,794 km)
Mass	1	About 10 Mars would equal the mass of Earth
Air	Oxygen and nitrogen	Carbon dioxide
Water	About 70% covered with water	Polar and underground ice, no liquid water
Moons	1	2
Potatoes	Earth has potatoes.	Phobos is shaped like a potato, but it is not a potato!

Glossary

asteroid A small rocky body that orbits the Sun.

canyon A deep, narrow valley with steep sides.

carbon dioxide A gas with no color that people breathe out and plants take in.

evaporate To change into a gas.

moon A body that circles around a planet.

orbit To travel around another body in outer space.

oxygen A colorless gas that humans and animals need to breathe that is essential to life.

planet A large body that revolves around a sun.

poles The farthest north and farthest south points of a planet.

rover A vehicle for exploring the surface of a planet or moon.

volcano A vent on the surface of a planet or moon through which lava from underground flows.

Read More

Aguilar, David A. *11 Planets: A New View of the Solar System*. National Geographic, 2008.

Cosson, M.J. *Your Mission to Mars*. Edina, Minn.: Magic Wagon, 2012.

Owens, L.L. *Mars*. Mankato, Minn.: Child's World, 2011.

Rusch, Elizabeth. *The Mighty Mars Rovers: The Incredible Adventures of Spirit and Opportunity*. Boston: Houghton Mifflin, 2012.

Sparrow, Giles. *Earth and the Inner Planets*. Mankato, Minn.: Smart Apple Media, 2012.

Websites

Mars Exploration Program: Mars for Kids
http://marsprogram.jpl.nasa.gov/participate/funzone/
Play a Mars adventure game, learn about the planet, and find out how much you would weigh on Mars.

Mission to Mars
http://athena.cornell.edu/kids/
The mission to Mars kids' page includes a day-by-day journal of Mars rovers, plus scientist profiles and FAQs.

Phoenix Mars Mission—Just for Kids
http://phoenix.lpl.arizona.edu/kids.php
Read about the Phoenix robotic lander, sent to study the Martian surface.

Welcome to the Planets: Mars
http://pds.jpl.nasa.gov/planets/choices/mars1.htm
View slideshows of the best photographs taken of Mars.

About the Author

Thomas K. Adamson lives in Sioux Falls, SD, with his wife, two sons, and a dog. He has written dozens of nonfiction books for kids, many of them about planets and space. He enjoys sports, card games, reading with his sons, and pointing things out to them in the night sky.

About the Illustrator

Daniele Fabbri was born in Ravenna, Italy, in 1978. He graduated from Istituto Europeo di Design in Milan, Italy, and started his career as a cartoon animator, storyboarder, and background designer for animated series. He has worked as a freelance illustrator since 2003, collaborating with international publishers and advertising agencies.